Oprah Winfrey

CINDY LEANEY

Level 2

Series Editors: Andy Hopkins and Jocelyn Potter

Pearson Education Limited
Edinburgh Gate, Harlow,
Essex CM20 2JE, England
and Associated Companies throughout the world.

ISBN 0 582 41982 4

First published 2000

Text copyright © Penguin Books 2000

Typeset by Digital Type, London
Set in 11/14pt Bembo
Printed in Spain by Mateu Cromo, S. A. Pinto (Madrid)

Published by Pearson Education Limited in association with
Penguin Books Ltd, both companies being subsidiaries of Pearson Plc

Acknowledgments:
All Action: pp. vi, 4, 7, 9, 14, 18, and 20; Rex Features: p. 12;
The Kobal Collection: p.16; Colorific!: p. 17

Every effort has been made to trace copyright holders in every case. The
publishers would be interested to hear from any not acknowledged here.

Contents

		page
Introduction		v
Chapter 1	A Child on a Farm in Mississippi	1
Chapter 2	Life with Mother	2
Chapter 3	"Out of a house, into a home"	3
Chapter 4	Difficult Years	5
Chapter 5	Life with Father	6
Chapter 6	The Early Days	8
Chapter 7	*The Oprah Winfrey Show*	11
Chapter 8	Reading	13
Chapter 9	Money	15
Chapter 10	Movies and Harpo	16
Chapter 11	Family and Friends	19
Chapter 12	The Woman Next Door	21
Activities		23

Introduction

There was no television in the house, but Oprah's grandmother taught her to read. She could read and write when she was only three years old. Her grandmother also taught her to pray.

Oprah's friends were the animals on the farm. She played with them and she read Bible stories to them.

Oprah Winfrey's story begins on a farm in Mississippi. She lived there with her grandparents when her mother went to work in another state.

When she was a child, she read all the time. Books were always an important part of her life. They showed her a world outside the farm.

Now she is very much a part of that world. She is rich and famous. People everywhere listen to her and love her.

Oprah works hard. She tries to be as good as she can be. This is her story.

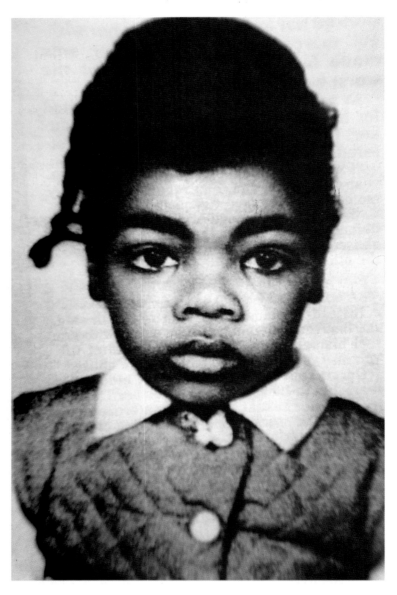

When Oprah was a child, she lived with her grandparents in Mississippi.

Chapter 1   A Child on a Farm in Mississippi

Vernita Lee met Vernon Winfrey in Mississippi one day in 1953. They were very young, and they were only together for a short time. They didn't marry.

Nine months later, on January 29, 1954, a baby girl was born. Vernita wanted to call her Orpah, a name from the Bible, but somebody made a mistake with the name. Oprah Winfrey's life began.

Vernita went north to Wisconsin and looked for work. She didn't take her baby with her because she couldn't clean houses with a child. She left Oprah with her parents—the child's grandmother, Hattie Mae, and her grandfather, Earless.

Hattie Mae was serious, strict, and very religious. Her husband, Earless, was a strange man. Oprah says that she was afraid of him.

The family didn't have much money. They ate the food from the farm. Oprah's grandmother made clothes for her. They worked and went to church. Oprah and Hattie Mae slept in the same bed. Earless slept in another room.

There was no television in the house, but Oprah's grandmother taught her to read. She could read and write when she was only three years old. Her grandmother also taught her to pray.

Oprah's friends were the animals on the farm. She played with them and she read Bible stories to them.

Oprah read and spoke in church. She wasn't afraid and Hattie Mae was proud of her. Oprah could do great things in life, she felt.

Many years later, Oprah said, "I started out speaking there."

Oprah's teachers loved her, but the children at church and

school disliked her. She was too smart and she could remember long Bible stories. They weren't kind to her.

Then, when Oprah was six years old, her mother sent for her. The child moved to a new life in Wisconsin.

Chapter 2   Life with Mother

Oprah was the only child on the farm. It was a quiet life out in the country with her grandmother, her grandfather, and the animals. Life in Milwaukee, Wisconsin, was very different.

Now she lived in a city with her mother and her half-sister, Patricia. They lived together in one room on a dirty, busy street.

Vernita worked a long way from home. She had to leave early in the morning and take buses across the city. She came back late at night, very tired. She didn't have much time for her children.

Oprah started at a new school in Milwaukee. She still loved books and she was intelligent. She did well and her new teachers liked her. But things were very different at home. The room was too small and Vernita had to make enough money for the three of them.

Patricia was a good, pretty little girl. Oprah was older and more difficult than her half-sister.

Vernita wanted to send Oprah back to the farm. But Oprah's grandmother was too old, and she couldn't look after the child. So Vernita asked Oprah's father for help.

Vernon Winfrey couldn't have children with his wife, Zelma. They wanted Vernon's child to live with them. So Oprah got on another bus and went south to her father's home in Nashville.

Chapter 3 "Out of a house, into a home"

Vernon worked hard. He had two jobs. He cleaned floors and worked in a kitchen. He and Zelma weren't rich, but they had enough money.

Oprah went to a new school in Nashville and she was a good student. But she had to do more than school work. At home, she had to read a book every week and write about it for Zelma. She also had to learn new words. Hattie Mae was strict, but Zelma was stricter.

Oprah worked hard at school and at church. When she was seven years old, she wrote a speech for a church. They paid her $500—a lot of money for a seven-year-old girl! But this girl was Oprah Winfrey.

It was her first "job." Young Oprah could write and speak well. Twenty years later, she wrote for radio and television. After that, she had a talk show.

It was a very busy year for Oprah. When summer began, she happily went to Milwaukee for the vacation. But at the end of the summer, Vernita wanted Oprah to stay in Milwaukee.

Vernon wasn't happy. He didn't want Oprah to stay with her mother. He said, "We brought her out of a house, into a home." Milwaukee was, he thought, not a good place for her.

Vernita had a new man. She wanted to marry him and start a better life. Another child was born—a son, Jeffrey—but Vernita's boyfriend didn't want to marry her. They all moved into a very small two-bedroom apartment together.

Oprah stayed in Milwaukee, but she wasn't happy there.

A young Oprah.

Chapter 4   Difficult Years

Oprah often thought about Vernon and Zelma. They were interested in her and gave her their time.

Oprah's mother was busy, and she had three children now. She showed her love in a different way—she worked hard for her children. But Oprah didn't understand that then.

A lot of different people came and went in the apartment—friends and family. When Oprah was twelve and thirteen, she had to sleep in a bed with her aunt's son, a fourteen-year-old boy. One night, he had sex with her. The next day, he bought her ice cream.

Oprah didn't tell anybody. There were other men—an uncle, then more boys. Oprah said later, "I wanted love and I looked in the wrong places."

At school, Oprah was more serious than the other students. Most of them didn't like her. They stopped her after school and they wanted to hurt her. She was afraid of them.

One teacher, Mr. Abrams, saw this. He was afraid for Oprah and wanted to move her out of the school. In 1968, he helped her go to a better, more expensive school.

The new school was a long way from the apartment, so Oprah went there by bus. The other people on the bus were women on their way to work.

The other students at school were mostly white, and they had a lot more money than Oprah. They lived in a different world. They had a lot of things, and Oprah wanted things too. She began to take money from her mother.

Then Oprah ran away from home. Vernita tried to put her into a home for problem girls. Oprah thought, "How did this happen? How did I get here?" But there wasn't enough room in the home for her at that time. They said, "Bring her back in two weeks."

Vernita couldn't wait, so she called Vernon in Nashville again.

He and Zelma still loved Oprah. They weren't rich but they had a small store. They had enough money and time for Oprah. Yes, Oprah could live with them.

Vernon drove up to Milwaukee and took his daughter home to Nashville.

Chapter 5   Life with Father

Oprah was fourteen now and she was a wild young woman. "You have to change," her father said. She couldn't wear short skirts. She couldn't stay out late. She had to study and work hard again.

Oprah wasn't stupid. She listened to her father and Zelma. They loved her and they wanted her to do well in life. She knew that.

Oprah started to dress and talk differently. She worked hard at school and was a good student again. At home, Oprah now had to read five books every two weeks and write about them for Zelma. She read books by slaves and other African-Americans. Oprah never forgot their stories.

In 1970, when Oprah was seventeen, she went to Los Angeles and made a speech at a church there. One afternoon, she visited Hollywood.

When she got back to Nashville, she said to her father, "I'm going to be famous." She wanted to be an actress. "One day," she

Oprah worked hard at school and was a good student.

told him, "my name will be there with other famous people, in front of Grauman's Chinese Theater."★

Oprah worked in her father's store after school and on weekends, but she hated it. She wanted something better.

One day, she went to a radio station. They asked her to read the news for them and she was very good. She got her first job in radio and they paid her $100 a week.

Oprah finished high school and started college. She didn't really like college, but she couldn't tell her father.

Next, a television station, WTVF-TV, asked Oprah to work for them. But Vernon wanted Oprah to finish college first.

One of her teachers said, "People go to college because they want good jobs." This was a very good job, Oprah thought. So she left college and took it.

No other woman or black person read the news on television in Nashville. The station paid her $15,000 a year. She was only nineteen years old at the time.

Chapter 6   The Early Days

Oprah worked at WTVF-TV for three years. She was good at her job and worked hard. She was warm and open and the people of Nashville liked her.

She still lived with her father and his wife. Her father was very strict; she always had to be home before midnight.

Then WJZ-TV television station in Baltimore gave her a job.

★ Grauman's Chinese Theater: You can find the names of very famous movie actors and actresses on the sidewalk in front of Mann's Chinese Theater in Hollywood. When Oprah was young, it was Grauman's Chinese Theater.

Oprah read the news and talked to people about their stories.

She was twenty-two years old and she wanted to live away from home now. So she went to live in Baltimore.

In Baltimore, Oprah read the news and talked to people about their stories. Sometimes the stories were very sad.

In one news story, seven children died in a house fire. Oprah had to talk to the mother of the children, but it was of course a very unhappy time for the woman. So Oprah didn't want to talk to her on TV. It wasn't right, she thought.

Oprah called WJZ-TV. "We can't use this story," she said.

"You're wrong. It's a good story," they told her. "You're too nice for television."

WJZ-TV took Oprah off the news.

But then, in 1977, Oprah started to do a talk show—*People Are Talking*. When she asked people questions, she was careful about their feelings. And she really listened to their answers. This was strange for a talk show, but it felt right to Oprah.

Debra DiMaio worked on the show. She said, "I never saw anybody work so hard."

Oprah showed *her* feelings. She laughed and cried with the guests on the show. They liked her, and the show was a big success.

Oprah did *People Are Talking* for six years. She wanted to talk to people in front of a TV camera and she wanted to be the best. She got better and better.

Oprah's love-life wasn't as good as her life at work. She was in love with a man, and he had a wife. She wanted to leave Baltimore. But where could she go?

Debra DiMaio now worked for a TV station in Chicago. She showed her new boss *People Are Talking*. He liked it and he wanted to meet Oprah.

Most of Oprah's friends didn't want her to move to Chicago. It wasn't a good idea, they thought. Only Debra and Oprah's best friend, Gayle King Bumpas, were happy about it.

Oprah says, "Chicago felt right. When I arrived, I knew that."

The people at the TV station liked her. Debra's boss said, "She was different from anybody on TV."

Oprah started doing the *A.M. Chicago* talk show on a very cold day in 1984. She had a new job and $200,000 a year. She was only twenty-nine years old.

Chapter 7 *The Oprah Winfrey Show*

In the beginning, the TV station gave Oprah boring questions for her guests. She had to ask, "What time do you get up in the morning?" or "What do you eat for breakfast?"

Oprah wasn't interested in the answers to these questions. So before people came on the show, she read about them. Then she asked them interesting questions about their lives. People really wanted to know the answers.

Oprah likes talking to people—famous or not. She had some very famous guests. She talked to Hillary Clinton, Sarah Ferguson, and Michael Jackson. She asked Brad Pitt, "What do you wear in bed?" And she asked Boy George, "What does your mother think when you wear women's clothes?"

She asked about feelings, family, and sex. She and her guests discussed a lot of different things. Many of these things were new to television talk shows.

Oprah is intelligent, funny, and warm. Guests say that they can talk to her easily. They are really open on her show. Oprah is very open about *her* life, too.

She first talked about her early sexual experiences on TV. She says it was good for her. It helped her understand her life. She was not the only child with these bad experiences.

Guests can talk to Oprah easily.

Oprah is not happy about some of her shows. Sometimes she asked dangerous questions. And sometimes she had dangerous guests on the show. On one show, she had people from the Ku Klux Klan.* She says that was a mistake.

Some talk shows want people to act strangely, so they pay them. Some shows want guests to fight on TV. They want guests to be wild or crazy.

Oprah isn't happy about those talk shows. Children come home from school and watch them. They teach children the wrong lessons.

The Oprah Winfrey Show is different. Oprah wants her shows to

---

* Ku Klux Klan: The Ku Klux Klan think that white people are better than African, Hispanic, or Asian people.

help people. "We want each show to open a door for somebody," she says.

Some people take time every day from their busy lives and think about the important things. They come on the show and talk about them.

People watch *The Oprah Winfrey Show* in more than 132 countries. Oprah says, "Television changes people's lives." Many people say that her show did change their lives.

Chapter 8   Reading

Reading is very important to Oprah Winfrey. Books opened doors for her. The little girl on the farm in Mississippi read the Bible. When she was older, Oprah read stories about slaves and other African-Americans. The rich, successful Oprah still reads a lot of books.

In 1996, Oprah started talking about books on her show. She wanted people to be excited about reading. She was very successful.

When she talks about a good book on *The Oprah Winfrey Show*, thousands of people buy it. There are study questions on the Internet. People can discuss the questions after they read the book. Many people write to her about the books. Sometimes she invites them on the show. Oprah also talks to the writers of the books.

Oprah discussed *The Song of Solomon*, by Toni Morrison, on her show. When Morrison heard about this, she wasn't very interested. But after the show, hundreds of thousands of people bought her book. They bought Morrison's other books, too.

Oprah is one of the richest women in the world. Her clothes are expensive and beautiful.

Chapter 9   Money

Oprah is one of the richest women in the world. She has a wonderful apartment in Chicago, and a farm and a house in the mountains. Her clothes are expensive and beautiful. She has great cars and an airplane, too.

"I love it. It's great!" says Oprah.

But money, she says, also gives you time for other, more important things.

Oprah likes to give things to friends and to people at work. Sometimes she gives them cars; sometimes she gives them money. One Christmas she gave $10,000 to some people at the TV station.

Dr. Maya Angelou, the famous writer, is a friend. "She is my mother, sister, friend," Oprah says. For Dr. Angelou's seventieth birthday, Oprah took her and some friends on a ship around Mexico for seven days.

She also uses her money for more serious things. She gives hundreds of thousands of dollars to students so they can go to college. She gives money to families so they can change their lives.

In 1997 she started Angel Network. This builds houses for people and gives away money across the United States. In 1998, it gave $25,000 to fifty high-school students for college. But many other people get money and help from Oprah. She doesn't talk about that.

Chapter 10   Movies and Harpo

The letters in Harpo, Oprah's company, are the letters of her name. When Oprah read the part of Sofia in *The Color Purple* for Steven Spielberg in 1985, she was very excited. The name of Sofia's husband in the movie is Harpo. She was happy about that.

The Color Purple, by Alice Walker, is a story about African-American women. When Oprah got the part in the movie, she said, "It's the happiest day of my life."

Oprah is a fine actress. Her next big movie part was Sethe, a slave woman, in *Beloved*. *Beloved* is a story from the 1800s. In the

Oprah is Sofia in The Color Purple.

Oprah is Sethe, a slave woman, in Beloved.

story, Sethe runs away. She doesn't want her children to be slaves, so she tries to kill them.

Oprah thought about Sethe for a long time before they started filming. Her friends took her out to the woods, because she wanted to understand the feelings of a slave. She wanted to experience those feelings. How did it feel when you ran for your life?

They put something over her eyes, so she couldn't see. Then they left her all night. Sometimes they went past her on horses and shouted at her.

She cried and cried that night. "I will never be the same again," she said.

Some parts of the movie were difficult for her. In the movie, Sethe puts her daughter to bed. That hurt Oprah, because her mother never did that for her.

Oprah and Stedman Graham are still together after many years.

Chapter 11   Family and Friends

Oprah says that her mother couldn't show her love. She feels sad about that. They were never a happy family. But she isn't angry now.

Oprah bought houses for her mother and half-sister, and she gives them money. She doesn't see her half-sister. Oprah says they have different ideas about right and wrong. Her half-brother, Jeffrey, died in 1989.

Gayle King Bumpas is Oprah's oldest friend. They met in 1976 when they were in Baltimore. They still talk on the telephone every day.

Oprah says, "We laugh every night about something."

Gayle has two children—a daughter, Kirby, and a son, William. They call Oprah "Auntie O."

Sometimes Gayle goes on *The Oprah Winfrey Show*. She can ask Oprah important questions about her feelings. Other people can't speak to her in the same way. Gayle asked the question about children.

"Are you going to have children?" she asked on a show about mothers. Oprah didn't answer. Then Gayle said, "Everybody wants to know the answer to that question!"

People also ask, "When will you marry Stedman?" There were other men in Oprah's life, but she and Stedman Graham are still together after many years.

He is a successful businessman. He is intelligent and kind. "And he's not famous!" says Oprah, happily.

She met him in 1985, but they never married. Will they marry someday? Everybody would like to know the answer to that question, too.

Oprah is now one of the most successful women in the world.

Chapter 12   The Woman Next Door

Oprah lives her life in front of a world of people. She is really open about her life, and her problems with food. When she has dinner in a restaurant, she can read about it in the newspapers the next day. Oprah's food is almost as important to the newspapers as her love-life.

She tried a lot of different diets. One year, she lost sixty-seven pounds. She came on her show with a jacket over her jeans. She took off the jacket and showed everybody the new Oprah. She was really proud. But the pounds came back.

Art Smith is Oprah's cook. He writes books and you can find him on the Internet at *oprah.com*. He helps Oprah with her diet. He helped her lose twenty pounds in one week. But she loves food, and dieting is very difficult for her.

Oprah is a very busy woman, but she tries to run every day. Bob Greene helps her plan her day. Then she can run before she goes to work.

Oprah is rich and famous, but she still has some of the same problems as the woman next door.

People watch Oprah and think, "She understands my life." They see a woman, not only a movie actress or a famous television face.

People listen to her and love her. She gets thousands of letters every week. Men and women, old people and children write to her. They tell her about their problems and their successes.

The little girl spoke at church. The young woman tried to find love in many different places. Oprah is now one of the most successful women in the world.

A road runs past her grandparents' farm in Kosciusko, Mississippi. Its name is now "Oprah Winfrey Road."

ACTIVITIES

Chapters 1–6

Before you read

1 What do you know about Oprah Winfrey? Write five things. What
do you want to ask Oprah Winfrey? Write five questions. Ask other
students your questions. Do they know the answers?

2 Answer the questions. Find the words in *italics* in your dictionary.
They are all in the book.

   a Do people *act* in a theater?

   b Do *feelings* come from your head?

   c When you are a *guest*, are you at home?

   d Do you find *news* in an old book?

   e Do people *pray* in a church?

   f Is *sex* a kind of restaurant?

   g Can you watch a *show* on television?

   h Is a *slave* a free person?

   i Do people listen to a *speech*?

   j Are you happy when you have a *success*?

3 Put these words in the sentences.

   enough   still   together

   a Is John . . . . . asleep?

   b Have you . . . . . money?

   c Shall we eat . . . . .?

4 What do you think? Are *you*:

   proud?   *religious*?   *serious*?   *strict*?

After you read

5 Can you answer any other questions from 1, above?

6 Who are these people? How were they important to Oprah?

   a Hattie Mae   **b** Mr. Abrams   **c** Patricia Lee

Chapters 7–12

Before you read

7 Find these words in your dictionary. Put them in the sentences.

   diet   experience   part

   a I got a ..... in a movie!
   b I can't eat it—I'm on a ......
   c Disneyworld was a great ......

8 What do you think will happen in Chicago?

After you read

9 Oprah moved to Chicago. How was her talk show there different from other talk shows?

10 Talk to another student.

   Student A: You work for a newspaper. What questions did you write before you read the book? Ask Oprah the questions.

   Student B: You are Oprah Winfrey. Answer the questions.

Writing

11 You work for a newspaper. Write about Oprah Winfrey's life before she went to Chicago.

12 You are Mr. Abrams. You want to help Oprah get into a good school. Write to the school about Oprah, the student.

13 You are a student. Angel Network gave you money for college. Write a letter to a friend. Tell your friend your feelings.

14 You want to be on *The Oprah Winfrey Show*. Write a letter to Oprah. Why do you want to be on the show? Tell her.

Answers for the Activities in this book are published in our free resource packs for teachers, the Penguin Readers Factsheets, or available on a separate sheet. Please write to your local Pearson Education office or to: Marketing Department, Penguin Longman Publishing, 5 Bentinck Street, London W1M 5RN.